Awaken
INSPIRED

PAGES FOR SELF EXPLORATION AND MOTIVATION

Dedication:

To *Gina Lisa* for being a constant light and giving me the push to go for it & live big, bold, and crazy. Thank you for reminding me that life is too short not to believe in yourself. And inspiring me to pass along the message...

To *everyone* who is looking to explore themselves, grow, and chase their dreams... I hope you finish these pages awakened and inspired.

CHAPTERS:

THE BASICS

PINPOINT YOUR DREAMS

MAKE YOUR GOALS A REALITY

MAINTAIN YOUR BALANCE

PAGES FOR EXPLORATION AND PROGRESS

JUST START

Because life is too short not to

BELIEVE IN YOURSELF

Introduction...

May your completion of this journal leave you more empowered than ever before. May you find your potential. Explore parts of yourself you have hidden away, may you find in yourself qualities you did not know were there and your soul become....awakened.

Within the depth of these pages allow yourself to be raw, vulnerable. Be your authentic self in order to find your alignment. There is bravery in exploring who you truly are. In feeling both the darkness and light inside of you.

Allow this journal to be your tool. To help guide you on your path to your awakening.

You are worthy. You are powerful. You can have it all.

The Basics

Peel back the layers, the definitions & labels,
Find Your True Self

WHO ARE YOU?

Your Name:

5 Words to *describe yourself*?

1
2
3
4
5

Which word do you like the _most_?

The _least_?

If you could adapt one word/quality you don't have yet _what would it be_?

Rank the words in order of
importance to you...

1

2

3

4

5

Where does the quality you want to adapt rank?

Which of these words give you the most pride?

Do any make you want to shed that layer & grow?

What is the next step?

Have you ever *hidden behind* or *adapted to fit* one of these words or *labels*?

How does that make you *feel*?

Feel these emotions & decide what you want to do with them...

Do you believe these words?

Are they what *other people* have *labeled you* Did you label yourself?

COME OUT OF HIDING!
Allow yourself to be free from the label...
THERE IS MORE TO YOU!

What is your favorite personality trait that you possess? Why is that? Where did you develop it from?

What is your *least* favorite thing about yourself?

What *emotions* did thinking about that bring up?

What is one *action* you can take daily to change that?

Let go of the things that do not bring you peace..

Do you *want to change* that?

Are you ready to *commit* to the *actions* you will need to take?

YOU ARE NOT STUCK
You hold the Power!

What steps are you taking to make that quality into something you love about yourself?

DO NOT HIDE!
Take this weakness and transform it into a strength

Grow & Adapt

Be proud of your process...

BE PROUD OF YOURSELF!

We all have the *Power* to transform

Find *Your* Starting Point

If you could tell the you from 5 years ago something what would you say?

What experiences shaped your answer?

What would you have done *differently* if you knew this then?

Would you have...
Lived more in the moment?
Dreamed bigger?
Taken more risks?
Played it safe?

Think of the *lesson* and how *truly strong* you are having *learned it*...

If you could tell yourself **anything** right now... *what would it be?*

Why did you pick that?

What are 10 things you are *grateful* for...

1.
2.
3.
4.
5.
6.
7.
8.
9.
10.

Today's date:

What are 3 things you are *Proud* of?

1.

2.

3.

What are your *greatest* accomplishments so far?

Don't be afraid to list both big & small...sometimes the smallest victories pave the way for the greatest moments!

Everything Matters!

What makes your *heart* beat faster?

DO MORE OF THAT

Do you do something you *love* everyday?

(Your job, a hobby, a project, etc.)

YES!   NO

What part makes you the happiest? How can you get more of that?

What do you need to do to make sure your days ALWAYS include something you love?

Do you need to make time for yourself? Start something new? Find a new job? Get a new hobby? MAKE A PLAN!

We all have the power to make our desires come to life...

you just have to be

BRAVE

enough to go after what you want!

Trust yourself

Take the leap!

A page to explore on a *rainy* day...
Circle the ones that fit your feelings

* The rain is calming; a relaxing white noise

* The rain is an annoyance & ruining my plans today

* The rain is washing away my struggles & anxiety today. It is giving me a fresh start.

* I prefer the sun

* The rain is giving me an excuse to relax today

What did you pick?

What is the rain *holding you back* from?

What is it allowing you to *escape*?

A page for a SUNNY day...how does sunshine make you feel? Are you *rejuvenated*? *Excited?* Ready to start a new day?

Does it make you want to stay inside & close the blinds?

How do you allow *external forces* to *influence* how you feel? How did your *mood change* from the sunny to rainy day?

You are in charge of what you give energy to...

Reflect on the last few pages... take note on how you <u>allow your environment</u> to influence your ==mood & perspective...==

Embrace your environment or have the courage to change it...

What is the most recent situation you have gone through that *forced you to grow*? To *change* your thought process or habits & *level up?*

How have you *changed for the better?*

CHALLENGES

come into our lives to help us *Grow*

...to push us

...to teach us

Learn the lesson

Feel what you need to feel and then remember your

STRENGTH

You are stronger than you know

What was the *hardest* situation you have gone through that taught you a lesson you will never forget?

No matter the circumstances involved...are you grateful for the lesson? Would you change it?

What are you AVOIDING?

Why are you running from it?

Give yourself the CREDIT

You deserve...

Make a word bank..fill it with characteristics you would use to describe yourself:

Are there any that you want to add? Write them here:

Which characteristics and qualities make you the most *proud?*

What actions can you take to strengthen those qualities?

5 Things that make you *happy*....

1.

2.

3.

4.

5.

How often do you get to enjoy the list on the previous page?

How can you change your daily habits to do these 5 things everyday?

Think about your daily routine. What is the best moment of your day?

How do you get more of that in your life?

It is easy to recognize the greatness in those you love...but often due to insecurities or fear it is harder for us to see the greatness within ourselves.

Think of the people you admire, who inspire you, make *a list of reasons why*...the qualities that stand out...

Now go back through the list & circle all the qualities that apply to you...

Do you possess most of the same ones? Do you *overlook* them in yourself and not acknowledge them as easily?

Characteristics

Who **inspires** you?

Why?

You have *Greatness* within you!

There is a part of yourself that you may not even have known existed

You have infinite power & potential inside of YOU

waiting to be explored

The time is now..peel back the layers. Break through it..explore the depth of who you are

Find Your Light

Exactly who you are is all you need to be

PINPOINT
YOUR
Dreams

10 Dreams you want to make come true...

1

2

3

4

5

6

7

8

9

10

Now *rank* the top 3...

1

2

3

What have you done *today* to make #1 *a reality?*

Put ACTION *behind your* DREAMS... Make them *come true!* You have the POWER!

What is the *first step* to making your dream happen...

What is holding you back?

Are you willing to *make the time* to chase your dreams daily?

What sacrifices are you willing to make to make your dreams come true?

List 3 *habits/actions* that are bringing you *closer to achieving* them?

1.

2.

3.

How often can you do the list above?

It's up to YOU to make time for *what matters!*

Finish this sentence:

No matter what I will...

I will not let _____

_____

STOP ME! I will...

What is your **Wildest** Dream?

DON'T HOLD BACK!

Sometimes the best ideas are the ones that seem the *craziest...*

YOU can do *Anything!*

A page for all of your *crazy ideas*

Sometimes the *best* ideas sound the craziest

Write freely...scattered... let your mind flow and see where it leads you...

This is the feeling I want to manifest in myself...

in others...

This is what I want to amplify...

I will bring it upon in *abundance*

Are there other avenues that will bring that feeling into your life? What steps can you take to pursue that feeling over & over...

EMBRACE YOUR PATH

YOU ARE ENOUGH. You have all you need within you to achieve *all* of your dreams. It is okay to want more. But always remain GRATEFUL for where you are in this moment. *Find the lesson.* You do not need to be or do anything people expect. Make your own rules.

you are in control.

But you have to believe it...

BELIEVE IN YOURSELF

You are *Limitless*

UNLOCK YOUR POTENTIAL
UNLOCK YOUR POTENTIAL
UNLOCK YOUR POTENTIAL
UNLOCK YOUR POTENTIAL

YOU HAVE THE
POWER
TO MAKE ALL OF YOUR
Dreams
COME TRUE

A page for your dreams...

Fill this page with *words of encouragement* — from yourself, friends, family, favorite quotes — if it means something to you ... write it down!

Now come back any time you need a reminder!

FIND YOUR FOCUS

Hold yourself accountable because _no one_ is going to do it for you.

What is your #1 goal?

When will you achieve it?
Give yourself a timeline, add check points to stay on track!

STEP >>>
OUTSIDE
OF YOUR
Comfort Zone

In pursuit of your goals...what makes failure *scary*? What are you afraid of?

If that happened — what would you do to overcome?

DOES IT MAKE IT LESS SCARY HAVING EXPLORED YOUR *plan of attack* FOR WHAT IS HOLDING YOU BACK? FOR YOUR FEARS...

FOLLOW THROUGH

When you don't want to that's when *you have to*...

REFLECTION...

What changes do you need to make to achieve your goals?

Are you on the right path? What actions are you taking?

Remember... without change there is no growth.

Describe your biggest *challenge* this past year..

How did you *overcome*?

NEWS FLASH

You will fail. You will faulter...it is inevitable.

BUT IT IS A TEST

HOW BAD DO YOU WANT IT?

HOW FAR WILL YOU GO TO CHASE YOUR DREAMS?

IT IS ALL ABOUT YOUR REACTION & THE ACTION YOU TAKE AFTER...

MAINTAIN YOUR *Balance*

YOUR BALANCE

Take the circle below — divide it into all sections you share your energy with... (yourself, family, friends, health, work, travel, financial, etc)

How much of your circle *energizes* you?
How much of it *drains* you?

Is there a *balance*? Is it *effortless*?

If you could *redirect* your time and energy, what would your circle look like? Would it change?

A page for *focus*...

Focus on this moment right now..live in it. *Cherish it.* Look around — enjoy. *Breathe*...take a moment for you. Describe where you are, physically... the sight, smells, your thoughts... emotionally... what are you *feeling*? What are you *fighting*? Be as detailed as possible.

What would you tell someone close to you that is chasing their dreams...

Now tell that to *yourself*...

A list of sacrifices I will have to make to achieve my goals...

Why I am okay with that...

What do you do when you get stuck & need a pick me up?

Who do you turn to? Yourself? A friend? Meditation? What brings you back?

YOU ARE *Supported*
YOU CAN DO ANYTHING!

When you are at your breaking point
Push past.. adapt and
GROW
Everything you face is meant to bring out the person you are *meant to be*!
The person inside of you is **stronger** than you realize. Let them lead the way! *Be all of who you are!*

Describe your biggest challenge at the moment...

How will you prevail?

What thoughts are circling back to you...
over & over...

Why is that? What is it *telling you*?

WHAT *lights* YOU UP?

EVERY MOMENT *Matters*

Take it all in..
own it..
live it..
embrace it.
All of it.
The calm. The storm.

What are 5 areas/things you want to _learn_ or _improve_?

1.
2.
3.
4.
5.

What are 3 _actions/steps_ you can take to achieve these?

1.
2.
3.

What parts of your life are *clashing* with what you want to achieve? What parts *compliment* it?

A page for love...

Write yourself a love note. Include all the things you love about yourself...all the things you are grateful for...

Speak your truth

Honor yourself...

Take a moment of *struggle* on your chase... remove yourself... step back & revisit the situation from *another point of view* —
WHAT IS IT TRYING TO TEACH YOU?

Don't take it personal...

These moments don't define you...

A page for reflection...

**What is *working* in my life?
What makes me excited? Laugh? Smile?**

How often do i get to *enjoy* these moments?

Do I need to do them more often?

Don't worry About the plan. **JUST TAKE ACTION.** No matter how small. The timing will never be perfect – *you may never feel ready*

TAKE THE LEAP

Trust yourself. Begin your journey. Don't let what you feel interfere with what you know. *Life is too short not to believe in yourself.*

TAKE ACTION
...and follow through

What are 3 things that you think of & instantly make you *smile?*

1

2

3

Are they habits? Situations? People? Places? How often do you get to *experience* or share your life with them?

Write out your daily routine...

Now circle all the parts that are bringing you closer to your goals...

Write down something you want to release in this moment. Something that is weighing you down...

A thought...
A feeling...
An energy...
A past experience

...anything

Now cross it out

over and over

YOUR SUPPORT SYSTEM

List all the people who *keep you going*.. don't forget **yourself**.. write a thank you to each one...

This is what I want to
RELEASE...

I WILL NO LONGER LET THIS WEIGH ME DOWN

Failure is *a part of the path* on your journey...
Write down anything you've tried, struggled with, not succeeded at...

Now decide which ones are *worth another shot!*
YOU'VE GOT THIS!

WHAT DO YOU NEED TO *remind yourself?*

A page for trying something new...

What is something you *tried for the first time*? Will you *do it again*? How did it *make you feel*? What gave you the COURAGE to try this?

BE PROUD OF YOURSELF.
New experiences bring new insight!

When you stumble - how do you *pick yourself back up*?

How do you not make the SAME mistake again?

PAGES FOR
Exploration
AND PROGRESS

Pages for Progress

What are 3 things you have done this week to bring you closer to your goal?

1. _____
2. _____
3. _____

CREATE HABITS TO MAKE YOUR DREAMS COME TRUE!

Check in... are you making the time to make it happen? What actions are you taking?

Pages for Progress

What are 3 things you have done this week to bring you closer to your goal?

1 _____

2 _____

3 _____

CREATE HABITS TO MAKE YOUR DREAMS COME TRUE!

Check in... are you making the time to make it happen? What actions are you taking?

Pages for Progress

What are 3 things you have done this week to bring you closer to your goal?

1 _____

2 _____

3 _____

CREATE HABITS TO MAKE YOUR DREAMS COME TRUE!

Check in... are you making the time to make it happen? What actions are you taking?

Pages for Progress

What are **3** things you have done this week to bring you closer to your goal?

1. _____
2. _____
3. _____

CREATE HABITS TO MAKE YOUR DREAMS COME TRUE!

Check in... are you making the time to make it happen? What actions are you taking?

PAGES TO TRACK YOUR PROGRESS

	Habit 1:	Habit 2:	Habit 3:
Monday			
Tuesday			
Wednesday			
Thursday			
Friday			
Saturday			
Sunday			

PAGES TO TRACK YOUR PROGRESS

	Habit 1:	Habit 2:	Habit 3:
Monday			
Tuesday			
Wednesday			
Thursday			
Friday			
Saturday			
Sunday			

PAGES TO TRACK YOUR PROGRESS

	Habit 1:	Habit 2:	Habit 3:
Monday			
Tuesday			
Wednesday			
Thursday			
Friday			
Saturday			
Sunday			

PAGES TO TRACK YOUR PROGRESS

	Habit 1:	Habit 2:	Habit 3:
Monday			
Tuesday			
Wednesday			
Thursday			
Friday			
Saturday			
Sunday			

IF NOT today... WHEN?

TAKE ACTION

MAKE YOUR DREAMS COME TRUE

WRITE YOURSELF A LETTER:

Today's date: _____

Dear _____

Just remember _____
_____
_____

With love, _____

Reflection:

THIS MONTH:

HAVE I STAYED COMMITTED TO TAKING ACTIONS/ STEPS TOWARD MY GOAL?

WHAT HAS KEPT ME ON TRACK?

WHAT HAS BECOME A DISTRACTION?

WHAT DID I LEARN?

WHAT ADJUSTMENTS DO I NEED TO MAKE?

Find Your Balance

THIS MONTH:

| Things I did and loved! & Would do again! | Things I did but did not enjoy. |

It is **your choice** where you spend your time & give your energy... do this every month until you are able to set boundaries & find balance.

Fill your life with momets that fill you up.

A PAGE FOR A DAY THAT WAS *Greater* THAN YOU COULD HAVE IMAGINED:

WHAT WILL YOU DO TO FEEL THIS WAY AGAIN?

A page for persistence

List **3** times the odds weren't in your favor.. but you persisted anyway. Did you prevail? What did you learn from each experience?

1

2

3

A page for Honesty

Go back and read your answers... have you responded with your raw, vulnerable, honest self? Or did you leave a guard up?

Make edits as needed. Write from the heart... raw...exposed...for yourself... **DON'T HOLD BACK**

What are you *resisting?* Allow it to be seen, hear your inner voice...

LET YOUR GUARD DOWN!

SAVE THIS PAGE FOR YOUR FIRST *Big Moment*

Today's date:

Now that you have achieved your goal... how do you feel? What emotions are surrounding you? What is running through your veins?

WHAT IS NEXT?

Bask in your accomplishment... feel the joy that comes with reaching a goal. But don't get content...keep moving towards greatness! Bring your power into the world! Share your gift!

www.ingramcontent.com/pod-product-compliance
Lightning Source LLC
Chambersburg PA
CBHW050302010526
44108CB00040B/2165